A SHORT GUIDE TO CAREW MANOR

compiled by
JOHN PHILIPS
based on research by the Carew Manor Group

London Borough of Sutton Leisure Services

First published 1989

London Borough of Sutton Leisure Services
The Old Court House, Throwley Way, Sutton, SM1 4AF
Telephone: 01-770 5000

ISBN: 0 907335 21 7

© Text: Carew Manor Group
Design: Shirley Edwards

ACKNOWLEDGEMENTS

This guide is based on the work of the Carew Manor group. The work would not have been possible without the sustained cooperation of the London Borough of Sutton, and in particular of Carew Manor School, over the last ten years.

ILLUSTRATIONS ACKNOWLEDGEMENTS

All illustrations are to be found in the Local Collection of the Heritage Service of the London Borough of Sutton, with the exception of the following, which are reproduced with the permission of the copyright holders as follows:

Front Cover:	© Judges Postcards Limited, Hastings, England.
Figure 1	Öffentliche Kunstsammlung, Kupferstichkabinett, Basel.
Figure 4	National Portrait Gallery, London.
Figure 15	© Crown copyright.
Figure 16	The British Library.
Figure 17	The Shaftesbury Society.
Figure 18	Greater London Photograph Library.
Figure 20	The Shaftesbury Society.

A SHORT GUIDE TO CAREW MANOR

THE CAREWS

Carew Manor is a fairly modern name for a building which was once known as Beddington Place or Beddington Park House. The present name derives from the Carew family, who owned the building and much of the surrounding land for several centuries.

The first Carew of Beddington was, like most of his successors, called Nicholas. He was a younger son with an insignificant inheritance who pursued a successful career in royal service and occupied the important office of Keeper of the Privy Seal from 1371 to 1377. He made enough money to be able to purchase a considerable, though scattered, estate which centred on Beddington.

He was succeeded in 1390 by his son, who was also called Nicholas, who made some additions to the estate but was less successful at court than his father. After his death in 1432, his successors did little more, and in the latter part of the 15th century the estate was administered on behalf of the young heir, who died within months of his coming of age in about 1485. After a legal dispute the estate was secured by his uncle, James Carew, who laid the foundations of the family fortunes in the Tudor period by an advantageous marriage. James's son Richard inherited in 1492, the year Columbus discovered America.

Richard never reached a very prominent position at court, but he was able to find the money for a substantial building programme. Some accounts survive from this period and show that work was being carried out on the north wing, and the core of the existing walls may date from this time. He is also known to have enlarged the deer park, and he is a possible builder of the Great Hall and its magnificent hammer-beam roof. If he did make the hall it was an extremely large and pretentious structure for a man in a comparatively modest position. He may have felt that it was justified by his ambitions for his son, another Nicholas. Richard managed to have him brought up with the young Prince Henry (later Henry VIII), and he could reasonably expect that the connection would be very profitable in later life.

His father's hopes in this direction were for a long time justified, as, apart from a few setbacks, Nicholas remained in favour and was a close companion of Henry VIII for many years. He received a succession of grants and offices, of which the most important were his appointment as Master of the Horse in 1522, and his admission to the Order of the Garter in 1536. Nevertheless, he eventually ended up on the losing side of the faction-fighting at court, and in 1539 he was executed for treason.

His property was forfeit to the crown and was added to the estates surrounding Henry VIII's palace of Nonsuch, on which construction had just started. This may have been an added incentive for Henry to send Nicholas to the block.

In Edward VI's reign the house was granted to Thomas, Lord Darcy of Chiche. Nicholas, however, had been a supporter of Mary, and shortly after she came to the throne she restored Beddington, and much other property, to Nicholas's son Francis.

Francis avoided open involvement in politics and seems to have had no difficulty in remaining in favour during Elizabeth's reign. His main interest appears to have been his garden, which was one of the finest in Elizabethan England. It is best described by Baron Waldstein, a German traveller who visited it in the summer of 1600:

1. Sir Nicholas Carew, K.G., (1527), from a drawing by Hans Holbein the Younger. Öffentliche Kunstsammlung, Kupferstichkabinett, Basel.

"We made a four mile detour via Beddington in order to see a most lovely garden belonging to a nobleman called Francis Carew. A little river runs through the middle of this garden, so crystal clear that you can see the water-plants beneath the surface. A thing of interest is the oval fish-pond enclosed by trim hedges. The garden contains a beautiful square-shaped rock, sheltered on all sides and very cleverly contrived: the stream flows right through it and washes all around. In the stream one can see a number of different representations: the best of these is Polyphome playing on his pipe, surrounded by all kinds of animals. There is also a Hydra out of whose many heads the water gushes"

The garden also contained orange trees which were covered by a removable wooden shed, or sheds, each autumn, and heated with stoves over the winter to keep the frost at bay. Orangeries later became very fashionable, but Francis's was probably the earliest in England and it was remarkable enough to be mentioned by many writers in the seventeenth and early eighteenth centuries.

Francis never married; and when he died in 1611 the house passed to his nephew, Sir Nicholas Throckmorton, who changed his name to Carew. He died in 1644, and was succeeded by his son, another Francis, who appears to have lost much of the family fortune by gambling, and by supporting the losing side in the Civil War.

In the second half of the seventeenth century there were two more long periods when the estate was inherited by a son too young to administer his own affairs. The house and

2. Sir Francis Carew (d.1611), from his tomb in Beddington Parish Church. Francis is chiefly remembered as the creator of the Elizabethan garden and orangery.

3. Sir Nicholas, 1st Baronet, who remodelled the house and garden at the beginning of the eighteenth century.

4. Admiral Sir Benjamin Hallowell Carew, from a portrait by John Hayter. National Portrait Gallery, London.

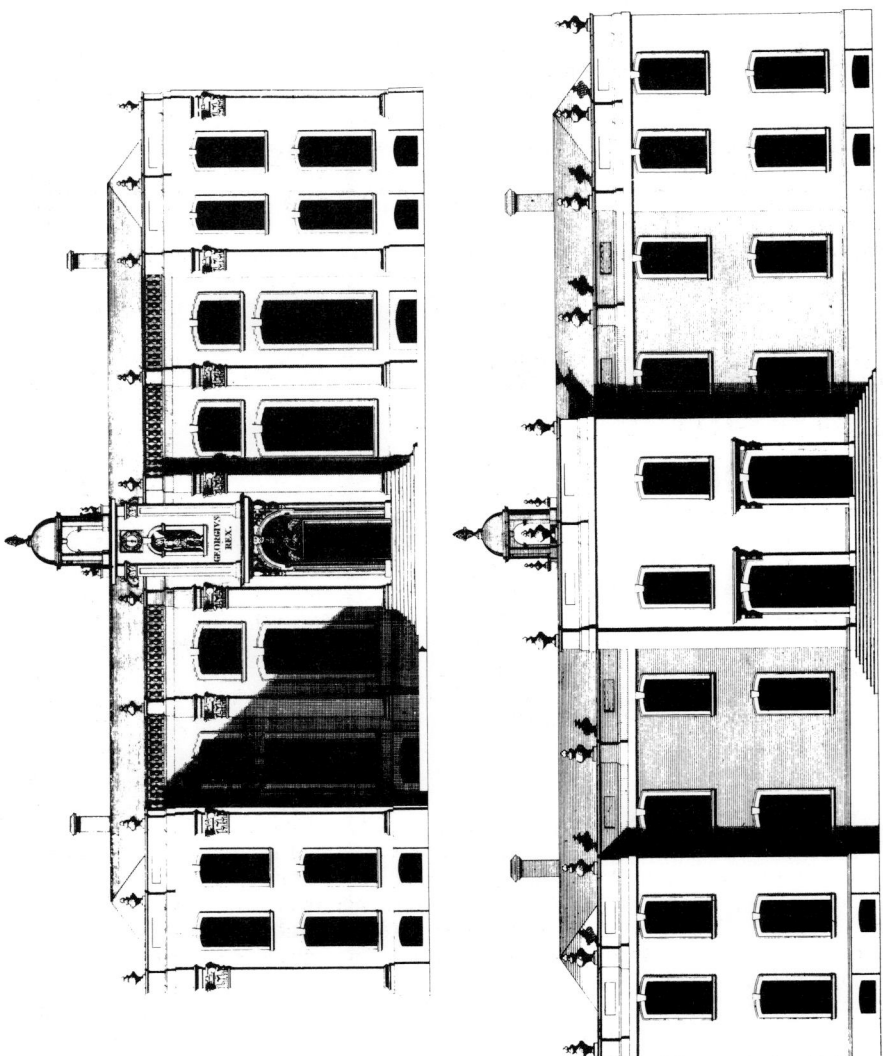

5. The west and east facades of the house, as published in Colen Campbell's Vitruvius Britannicus of 1717. TOP: Front view (west elevation). BELOW: Rear view (east elevation). These give a good impression of the house after the early eighteenth century remodelling, bearing in mind that Campbell omitted most of the chimneys and falsified other details in order to present the appearance of perfect symmetry.

gardens were neglected and in poor condition when the ninth Nicholas (later created first Baronet) came of age in 1707. His modernisation of the house included the classical façade shown in engravings by Colen Campbell. He also made extensive alterations to the garden and constructed the surviving Orangery Wall.

Nicholas died in 1727 and was followed by his seven-year-old son, the tenth and last Nicholas and the second baronet. He was financially inept, and there are references to unpaid debts and to the sale of some of the family silver.

After his death, in 1762, the property passed to his daughter Catherine, who died unmarried in 1769. The estate then passed to the Gee family, who were related to the Beddington Carews two generations back; and then, in 1828, to Benjamin Hallowell, who adopted the Carew name, but had no blood relationship with the original line. He had been born in Canada and served in the navy with Nelson. He reached the rank of Admiral by the time he retired in 1830.

His grandson, Charles Hallowell Hallowell Carew, gambled himself into bankruptcy. The estate was sold in 1859, and the house passed to the Lambeth Female Orphan Asylum, which later became the Royal Female Orphanage Asylum. The orphanage was evacuated in the Second World War and did not return.

In 1954 the house became a school run by Surrey County Council. This was taken over by the London Borough of Sutton in 1965, and continues to occupy the building.

THE GREAT HALL

The most striking feature of the Great Hall is its arch-braced hammer-beam roof (see diagram (figure 11)). The hammer-beams are the horizontal timbers which project inwards from the top of the wall. The timbers which rise vertically from the ends of them are called hammer-posts, while the arch-braces are the long curved pieces of timber which run from the wall, through the hammer-beams, to meet the collars in the centre of the hall.

Hammer-beam roofs were quite widely used in the late medieval and Tudor periods. Examples can be seen in many East Anglian churches; at some Oxford colleges; in the halls of the royal palaces at Westminster, Eltham and Hampton Court; and elsewhere. There is considerable variation in both structure and decoration. The roof at Beddington looks very similar to that at Eltham in Kent, which was erected in the late 1470s as part of Edward IV's remodelling of the palace. The resemblance is, however, only superficial, as the structure of the Beddington roof is very unusual. Barry Weston, a keen local archaeologist, has studied the roof and found that it is made of small carved pieces of wood applied to an underlying timber frame. The arrangement of the frame is shown in figure 11 which also shows the normal structure of a hammer-beam roof.

At Beddington, the hammer-post is made of two pieces of timber, and the curving arch-brace passes between them. Normally the brace would continue downwards until it meets the wall post, but, at Beddington, it bends to one side and joins the underside of the rafter. The original line of the brace is continued with a separate piece of wood.

From within the hall all this is hidden, as the main timbers are covered with the mouldings, which give a false impression of thickness. The timbers which bend aside to meet the rafters are concealed behind plaster panels. This structure is highly eccentric, and is, so far as we know, unique, and its reason is a mystery; although it allows the use of smaller, and therefore cheaper, timber.

There appears to be a decorative moulding along the outer edge of the hammer-posts which is largely concealed by other mouldings laid on top of it. This strange arrangement may suggest that the design of the roof had been altered at some stage early in its life.

The stone corbels which appear to support the roof are another puzzling feature. The

6. The east front of the house in the mid-nineteenth century, from an engraving by Joseph Nash. This side of the house had been little altered since the early eighteenth century. The beds and walks of the early eighteenth century garden had been covered with grass; and the east lake, which can be seen in the foreground, had been partly filled to produce a more natural, curved edge.

7. A print by Nathaniel Whitlock, c. 1830, showing the west front of the house and the church of St. Mary the Virgin. The end of the west lake can be seen in the foreground.

11

8. LEFT: The hall interior in the mid-nineteenth century from a lithograph by Joseph Nash, showing the decoration and panelling made for the first baronet in the early eighteenth century.

9. RIGHT: The plaster panel in the Great Hall with the achievement of arms of Sir Nicholas Carew, first Baronet. This can be seen on the end wall in the Nash lithograph.

only finished corbel is in the north-east corner: the others become progressively less complete towards the south end of the hall, suggesting that the work came to a premature halt, although again the circumstances surrounding this are unknown.

What did the interior of the hall originally look like? An idea can be formed from documents and from comparisons with other halls of a similar age. The existing windows are Victorian. In medieval halls the windows were generally set high, and the lower part of the wall was covered with panelling or tapestry. The existing panelling is also Victorian, but accounts show that there was panelling in the hall in the sixteenth century.

10. A drawing by Joseph Nash of some early sixteenth century panelling which survived in the house into the nineteenth century. This was probably destroyed during the conversion into an orphanage in the 1860s.

The south end of the hall would have been divided off by a wooden screen similar to the one which still exists at Penshurst Place in Kent. A passage would have run across the hall behind the screen with the main outside door opening into one end of it. The screen probably had three openings which were matched by three doors on the opposite side of the passage in the south wall of the hall. The two doors at each side opened into the pantry and buttery, from which food and drink were served, while the middle door provided a route to the kitchen. The screen was generally only half the height of the hall, and there was often a gallery above the screen passage from which musicians could play during meals.

At the other end of the hall the floor was usually raised slightly to make a low platform, or dais. There would have been a large open hearth in front of this from which smoke would drift up until it found its way out through a louvre in the roof. The louvre is mentioned in some sixteenth century accounts, and two timbers which probably supported it can still be seen running across the roof, near the apex, in the second bay from the north end of the hall.

The hall was redecorated by the first baronet at the begining of the eighteenth century. He covered the floor with black and white stone slabs, put up new panelling and covered the upper part of the walls with decorative panels. The centre pieces were two moulded plaster panels on the end walls of the hall which still survive. One contains his achievement of arms, whilst the other is known as a 'trophy' which incorporates the initials of himself and his wife Elizabeth Hacket cut into the armour, as well as the Carew and Hacket banners crossed.

Most of this decoration was destroyed when the house was converted into an orphanage in the late 1860s. The eighteenth century panelling was removed and replaced by the existing cheap panels, and a large part of the upper wall was replastered.

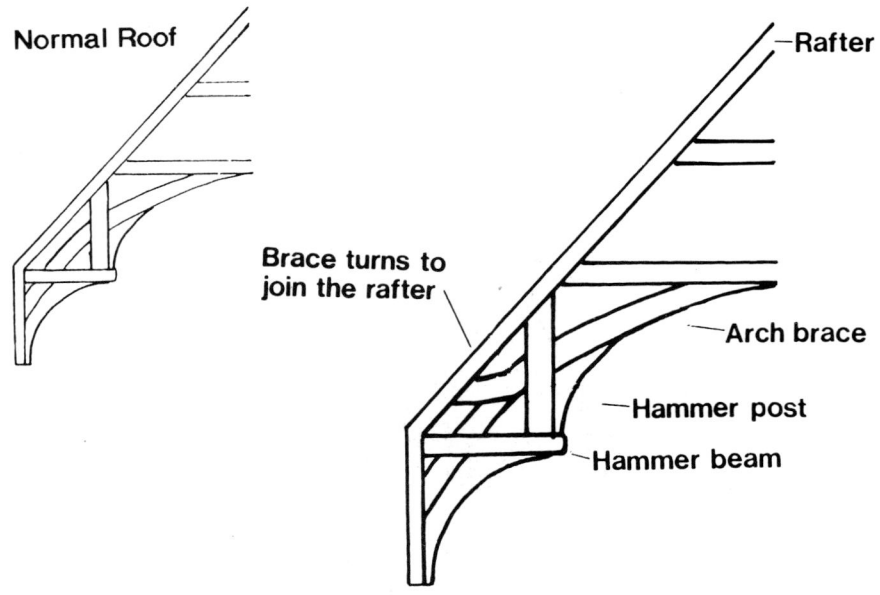

11. The structure of a hammer-beam roof. LEFT: A diagram of normal roof structure. RIGHT: A diagram showing the various elements of the roof structure in the Great Hall.

12. TOP: *The roof of the Great Hall.*

13. BELOW: *Part of the north end of the Great Hall roof, seen from the attic of the north wing. A is the rafter; B is the hammer-post; C is the hammer-beam; D is the arch-brace which bends to meet the rafter; and E continues the brace. (See also figure 11.)*

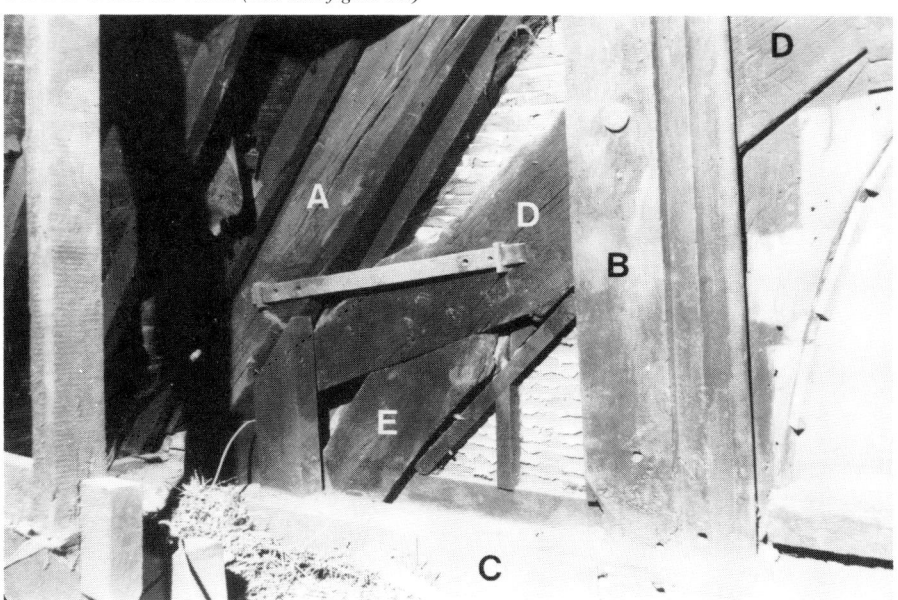

15

THE CELLARS

Apart from the Great Hall, the most important remains in the house are to be found in the cellars. Like the rest of the building these have been much altered, and include fragments from many different periods. The most interesting features can be seen under the south-east corner of the building, beneath what was the kitchen block of the Tudor house. Here there is a well-preserved Tudor doorway, and a wall of flint and earth which predates the Tudor period. This is almost certainly the earliest visible structure in the house. One of the cellar passages, which was cut through the foundations of the kitchen in the 1930s, broke into the arched top of a chamber which is now earth-filled. This lay under the former kitchen and may have been a well, or water storage cistern, as a inventory of 1762 says that the kitchen contained "a lead pump with its apparatus at the End of the Cistern with a lead pipe down to the arch . . . ".

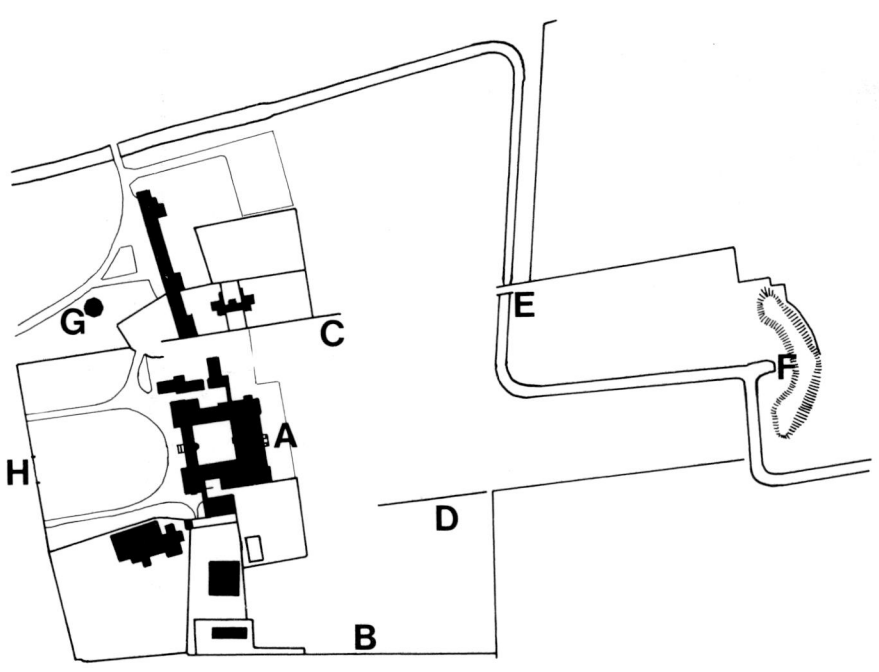

14. The location of features in the garden. A is the starting point for the tour; B the Tudor boundary wall; C the site of the northern gates; D the Orangery Wall; E the bridge over the Wandle; F the site of the culvert; G the dovecote; H the start of the Beddington Park Heritage Trail.

THE GARDEN

The only standing remnant of the Elizabethan garden is the boundary wall along Church Lane (figure 14B) but there are substantial remains of the garden laid out by the first baronet at the beginning of the eighteenth century. The best starting point for a tour of these is at the doors to the Great Hall on the east side of the house (figure 14A).

Standing here at the beginning of the eighteenth century, and looking away from the house, you would have had a view down the centre of the main garden, which was bounded by brick walls on both north and south sides. Only a short section of the northern, or left-hand, wall survives, which includes two pillars which once supported a set of ornamental wrought iron gates. A drive ran across to a matching pair of gates on the opposite (southern) side. The pillars which supported these have now gone, but a photograph of them taken in the nineteenth century is reproduced (figure 17).

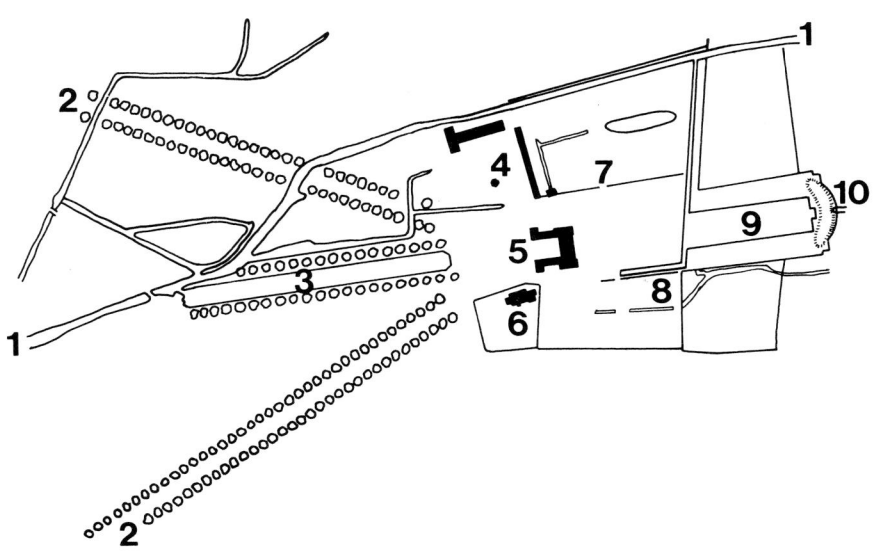

15. A tentative reconstruction plan of the early eighteenth century garden, based on the 1956 O.S. map, scale 25" to 1 mile. 1 The river Wandle; 2 the avenues of trees radiating from the front of the house; 3 the west lake lined with trees; 4 the dovecote and other outbuildings; 5 the house; 6 the church; 7 the north gates; 8 the Orangery Wall; 9 the east lake; 10 the curved bank with a cascade in the centre.

17

South East View of Beddington Park, Surrey; the Seat of Mrs Gee. June 1st 1827.

16. The south-east corner of the house in 1827, from a drawing in the British Library. Note the Tudor chimneys on the roof. The gothic windows in the south wing (on the left) date from a modernisation of 1818, while the east front (on the right) dates from the early eighteenth century.

The fine brick structure just beyond the site of the gates is known as the Orangery Wall (figure 14D). The north side of this, which can be seen from the house, is divided into nine sections by rectangular columns or pilasters. These, and the doorway at the east end of the wall, have been beautifully made: the bricks were fitted together as closely as possible, with capitals and other decoration carved in the brick and rubbed smooth. The doorway is now sadly battered, but a photograph taken some years ago gives an idea of its former appearance (figure 18). At the beginning of this century the doorway opened into a lean-to which was built against the south side of the wall. This replaced an earlier structure which may have had a connection with the Beddington Orangery. The lean-to was part of a series of sheds built up against the wall in the 1870s, used for storage and stabling horses.

It is often said that the first oranges in England were grown at Beddington during the reign of Elizabeth 1. This is certainly untrue, as there are occasional references to orange trees in England in the Middle Ages. However, Francis Carew, who owned the house in the Elizabethan period, was almost certainly the first person to grow them in England on a

17. The wrought-iron gates on the south side of the garden, near the Orangery Wall, c.1907. The gates are now at the Huntington Museum in California.

19

18. The doorway in the Orangery Wall, from a photograph taken c.1950.

large scale. He visited Paris in 1561—2 and is known to have bought trees there. It is likely that some of these were oranges and that the building was erected shortly after he returned. The earliest known reference to it, however, is in the household accounts for the 10th January 1608, when a man called Sadler was paid for sweeping snow from its roof.

The orangery became quite famous so there are a number of references to it in the seventeenth and early eighteenth centuries which give us some idea of its appearance. In 1700 John Evelyn said that "the oranges were planted in the open ground & secured in winter onely [*sic*] by a Tabernacle of boards, & stoves, removable in summer . . .". In 1652 a carpenter was paid £60 for a new orange house — probably really an extension of the existing one —and there were also payements for mending and enlarging the iron stoves which were used for winter heating . The original building was therefore a wooden structure and there is no mention of either brickwork or a wall. In 1691 an otherwise unknown J. Gibson reported that the house was above two hundred feet long and that most of the trees were thirteen feet high.

The style of the existing wall suggests that it was built about 1700, and it is almost certainly the work of the first baronet (1707—27). The original trees are said to have survived until the winter of 1739—40, and the wall may have been constructed as a shelter

20

along the north side of them, although there can be no certainty about this, as the wall and the orangery are only linked by tradition.

The eastern end of the garden is best examined by walking along the side of the hedge; crossing the bridge over the river at the corner of the housing estate; (figure 14E) and then going up to the large cedar tree (figure 14F) which may be about 200 years old.

The tree stands on an earth bank which was backed by a curving brick wall, of which the northern half survives. The river originally entered the garden through two culverts in the centre of the bank and flowed over a low cascade into a lake. The cascade has now gone, but the ends of the culverts can still be seen. At the begining of the nineteenth century the lake had a T-shaped plan with curving corners, but archaeological evidence suggests that it was originally more rectangular (figure 15).

In the eighteenth century the river appears to have flowed from the lake roughly along the line of the present channel under the foot bridge (figure 14E). The alignment of the channel is echoed in the stone capping of the pillar which stands by the bridge. The pillar was formerly part of the wall along the north side of the main garden.

THE DOVECOTE

The brick-built octagonal dovecote was built around 1715—20, and replaced an earlier building. It is exceptionally large and contains over 1200 nesting boxes, built into the inner face of the wall. These were used by the pigeons or doves, which came and went through the wooden turret at the apex of the roof. The central vertical post and arm are the principal members of the large rotating ladder, called a potence, which gave access to the nesting boxes, which were raided for both eggs and nestlings, known as 'squabs', which provided meat for the manor house table. Any surplus may have been sold at market. The bird droppings which accumulated on the floor may also have been collected and sold, since they contained saltpetre which could be extracted and used as the oxidising agent in gunpowder.

BEDDINGTON PARK COTTAGES

The row of cottages to the east of the dovecote are a modern (1986) rebuilding of a range of derelict farm cottages, which had been rebuilt piecemeal from a long outbuilding, which ran north to south facing the dovecote. Until 1986 the most northerly units had a substantial timber-frame, with a crown-post roof, and represented the surviving end of the longer structure, dating probably from the late fifteenth or early sixteenth centuries. A few fragments of the original timberwork can still be seen, mixed with modern timbers, on the north wall, by the bridge over the river.

19. The early seventeenth century orangery at Heidelburg in Germany. The sixteenth century orangery at Beddington was probably similar to this.

20. The east lake with the cascade in the background. This photograph was taken when the orphanage occupied the house.

21. View down the west lake towards the house, taken from the 1859 sale catalogue.

22. The exterior of the dovecote.

THE PARK

23. The interior of the dovecote, showing the central rotating ladder, or 'potence', and the nesting boxes built into the wall.

Beddington Park is a fragment of a large deer park which was once attached to the house. At the end of the sixteenth century it covered about 575 acres and extended northwards to the edge of Mitcham Common. We do not know who first made the park, but Sir Richard Carew is known to have extended it while he owned the house (1492—1520). In the sixteenth century it would have consisted of a mixture of woodlands, and grassy areas, which provided grazing for the deer. The park was surrounded by a pale, which was a substantial wooden fence, usually with a ditch on the inside to make it difficult for the deer to jump out. At some time in the seventeenth or eighteenth century the northern part of the park was divided into fields, probably in one of the many periods when the family was short of money. When the Carew estates were sold in the mid-nineteenth century, the existing park was bought by Canon Alexander Henry Bridges, who was rector of Beddington, and who spent part of his large fortune on public amenities and on improvements to the church. Most of the remainder was bought by the Croydon Sanitary Authority and used as a sewage farm.

The modern park contains many historic features. The London Borough of Sutton Leisure Services has recently made a heritage trail around it which can be followed from the iron gates in front of the house (figure 14H). A separate leaflet is available which describes the trail in detail.